MAIDSTONE
PAST & PRESENT

RICHARD STUTELY

COUNTRYSIDE BOOKS
in association with
MAIDSTONE MUSEUMS & ART GALLERY

First Published 1986
© Maidstone Museums & Art Gallery 1986

COUNTRYSIDE BOOKS
3 CATHERINE ROAD
NEWBURY, BERKSHIRE

ISBN 0 905392 74 4

Produced through MRM (Print Consultants) Ltd, Reading
Typeset by Acorn Bookwork, Salisbury
Printed and bound in England by Borcombe Printers, Romsey

INTRODUCTION

Most people enjoy looking at old photographs of their town, especially if those photographs evoke pleasant personal memories. 'Ah yes', they say, 'My sister got married in that church and I used to sing in the choir'; 'my first job was at Blake's in the High Street; I was fourteen then'.

There is nothing quite like an old photograph of something familiar to trigger a bout of nostalgia. Even while selecting these photographs from the large collection in the museum archives I was reminded of a previously-forgotten aspect of my early schooldays when I found an old view of the swimming baths, then located in Fairmeadow near the river. Once a week we village children were brought to the 'Big Town' for our swimming lessons and that photograph suddenly brought back to me the feeling of excitement I used to experience as the coach turned left off the bridge and into the gloomy industrial canyon that was Fairmeadow in the early 1950s. Ah yes, there was also the smell of gas and beer mash in the air, the whiff of chlorine and the sustaining iced bun in the cafeteria after the swim.

Yes, an old photo can be a powerful stimulus to the memory. I hope these photographs will not only bring back memories but help to show to newcomers and the younger generation some of the changes that have occurred in the town over the last one hundred or so years. There have been quite a few.

Maidstone's early history does not really concern us here; it is excellently documented elsewhere. Suffice to say that the town began around the time of the Norman conquest as a manorial estate under the control of the Archbishop of Canterbury. The Church played an important part in the town's early development. The fine group of old buildings around All Saints' church bear witness to that fact.

Despite supporting several rebellions and taking the Royalist side in the Civil War, Maidstone grew into a prosperous market town with several important industries. Its central position in the county of Kent, known even in Tudor times as the Garden of England, and the fact that the river was navigable and provided ready access to London, helped greatly. By 1821, the census showed a population of 12,508 mainly concentrated around High Street, Week Street, King Street and Union Street. About this time gas was introduced to the town and two years later the Maidstone Gas Light and Coke Company was set up by Act of Parliament. The works, in St Peter's Street, remained until the introduction of North Sea gas in the 1970s. The retort houses and ovens are now demolished, leaving only a solitary gasometer and the Segas offices.

The electricity works stood on the opposite bank of the river, in Fairmeadow. It opened in 1901 and was operated very efficiently by Maidstone Corporation for forty-seven years before passing to national control. The whole of Fairmeadow has now been cleared of buildings and provides public access to the river.

Maidstone's situation in one of England's major hop growing areas certainly helped the development of breweries in the town. There were three down by the river, providing employment for many people over the years. Recent rationalisation and the problems of effluent mean that actual beer production has gone elsewhere, but both Whitbread-Fremlins and Courage have retained distribution depots within the Borough.

What about transport? Well, Maidstone did resist the railways until 1844, when a branch line was opened to Paddock Wood. The feeling was that these new-fangled trains would damage trade on the Medway. However, the town ended up with four railway stations, if the Barracks and Tovil are included, and so honour was satisfied.

The motor car did little to help the town, though. The main A20 trunk road to the coast passed straight through the town centre. Memories of snarl-ups on the bridge still bring a look of fear to the eyes of veteran drivers, but the opening of the by-pass in 1960 certainly helped. Maidstone was the first town in Kent to adopt parking meters! There is still far too much traffic passing through the town centre and hopefully the projected road improvements will bring some relief in the 1990s.

But what of Maidstone today? The last census figures show that the Borough had a population of almost 130,000 and the town is one of the most prosperous in the south east. Few would dispute that the riverside area is greatly improved, and will be improved further when the old gasworks site is redeveloped. We escaped, by and large, the wholesale bulldozing that befell many town centres thirty years ago. The High Street has probably never looked better and several seedy areas have taken on a new lease of life. We still have our problems, but what town does not. Few would deny that Maidstone has stepped into the 1980s with dignity.

Due credit should be given to those early photographers whose work is reproduced in this book. Unfortunately their names are not recorded on the majority of the prints used here; at least not on the museum's copies. There is also a paucity of accurate dates, leading to the ubiquitous c. for circa in cases where definite dating has proved difficult. Of those photographers whose work can be identified I must mention the partnership of De'ath and Dunk; I only wish I could begin to approach their standards.

My friends at Maidstone Reference Library proved, as ever, of great assistance, especially at a time when the Museum's library was inaccessible. Their collection of local newspapers is invaluable to all aspiring local historians.

Certainly Allen Grove, a curator of the museum for over twenty five years, deserves credit. He knows so much about Maidstone and although now retired has helped me many times over the years with difficult queries. Last but not least, Mrs Eve Wells did an excellent job of typing up the text.

All photographs are reproduced by kind permission of Maidstone Borough Council.

Richard Stutely

CONTENTS

HIGH STREET 1904

THE WIDE upper High Street which once housed the town's markets is dominated by the monument to Queen Victoria. This incorporated a drinking fountain and was presented to the town by local banker Alexander Randall in 1862. A waiting horse cab can be seen behind the monument.

TAXIS STILL wait behind the monument, and the buses, which stop opposite, tend to pollute the air with their diesel fumes. Horses had pollution problems too; something we tend to forget. Keeping the hems of long dresses clean must have been a real problem.

THIS MOCK TUDOR building at the west end of Middle Row was the Electricity Board showrooms at that time. Earlier, the Maidstone Gas Company had a shop there.

HIGH STREET 1986

THE IMPOSING Barclays Bank building, built in 1963, has sculptured depictions of pre-decimal and 17th century coins in relief on the end wall. To the left, at the junction of Pudding Lane, the former Chiesman's department store has now closed and has been converted to smaller shop units.

HIGH STREET
c. 1915

GEORGE MENCE SMITH'S household supply shop at no. 19 High Street sold a wide range of goods including groceries, paints and ironmongery. The two girl assistants standing in the doorway here were known as the 'Paraffin Queens'.

HIGH STREET 1986

NO. 19 IS NOW part of a card shop. The exterior certainly looks bare compared to the earlier photograph.

HIGH STREET c. 1930

HIGH STREET, MAIDSTONE (12)

THIS PHOTOGRAPH, taken from the Town Hall roof, shows the old-established shop of Haynes Brothers Ltd, on the corner of Week Street and King Street. The Red Lion public house, known locally as the Gin Palace because of its special bar for ladies only, stood on the corner of Week Street and High Street just above the Westminster Bank. The spire of Holy Trinity church, now closed, can be seen rising above the skyline.

12

HIGH STREET 1986

THE SAME VIEW is now completely dominated by Colman House, an eleven storey office block which says much about the 1960s style of architecture. Haynes Corner was demolished and widened out for a row of shops, but the old Red Lion building remains and is now a clothing store.

13

THIS BEAUTIFUL BUILDING, known as Bliss's House, stood in the lower part of the High Street, on the south west side. It was demolished in 1871 to make way for the new main post office. The decorated plasterwork, known as pargetting, was regarded as some of the finest in England. Unfortunately none of it was salvaged.

14

HIGH STREET 1986

THE MAIN POST OFFICE at no. 58 was moved to its present position in King Street in 1928 and the building was then used for the County Court offices. Dickinson's printing works was next door and the legend 'printing works' is still above the entrance. Fire recently destroyed the adjacent shops, which are now being rebuilt, and the whole block is being given a facelift.

15

HIGH STREET c. 1860

THESE 15TH CENTURY houses stood just below the Royal Star Hotel; the brick façade of the hotel is just visible on the right hand side of the picture.

BANKS AND building society offices predominate in this area and the Royal Star Hotel has now shut, to be replaced by a shopping arcade behind the original exterior. The Star was originally a coaching inn, but most people will associate it more with lively Saturday night dances held in the large function room at the rear of the building.

THE SUN INN, half way along Middle Row, dates from the 16th century. The landlord, Claude Porter, whose name is prominently displayed above the entrance, was a colourful character with a penchant for maroon cars and matching suits. An earlier landlord had the apt name of Boozer.

THE SUN remains much as it was, and so far has not suffered a trendy name change or developed a 'theme' to suit the tastes of the younger customers.

HIGH STREET c. 1900

BLAKES LADIES OUTFITTERS at 93–94 High Street occupied an interesting iron-framed building dating from 1855. In 1836 there was a plan to build a railway station on a site slightly farther towards Bank Street but this was opposed on the grounds that a railway might damage the river trade.

THE IRON-FRAMED BUILDING, attractively restored, now serves as a branch of the Royal Bank of Scotland.

YE OLDE STORES, Tom Button's shop at the bottom of Gabriel's Hill specialised in perambulators, bedsteads, general furniture and servants' boxes in wood and iron. It was demolished in 1936.

A FAIRLY uninteresting block of shops and offices replaced Button's premises and the attractive Georgian brewery house which stood farther along in the continuation of Lower Stone Street. Water Lane, which until recently ran off to the left of the picture, has now completely disappeared under the Stoneborough Centre.

GABRIEL'S HILL c. 1900

ANOTHER VIEW of Button's shop on the right. Farther up on the left is a white building, then occupied by Sibley & Co., motor car and cycle factors. This was later rebuilt as the Maidstone Palace of Varieties theatre, which opened on 23rd March, 1908. One of the first acts to appear was Harry Lauder.

GABRIEL'S HILL 1986

THE PALACE THEATRE ended its days rather ignominiously in the late 1950s, when it was reduced to showing naturist films and staging piano playing marathons. It was demolished to make way for a Sainsbury's supermarket, later to be replaced by an ironmongery chain store. The large gilt top boot still hangs on a scrolly iron bracket to advertise the shoe shop below, whilst the Ship Inn enjoys a new lease of life as a wine bar!

KING STREET 1902

MOST OF THESE old houses were demolished in 1927 when King Street was widened. One of them was the birthplace in 1735 of William Woollett, who became one of the most successful line-engravers of his time. Woollett was later appointed 'Engraver to George III' and his name is commemorated in Woollet Street, near to the prison.

THE SAME CORNER now bears little resemblance to the earlier photograph. King Street was originally called East Lane, and the name was changed to mark the visit of George III to the town in 1799. He came to review a large force of volunteer troops which had been assembled on Lord Romney's land at Mote Park.

KING STREET c. 1911

THE DOG AND BEAR pub once stood on the other corner of the Church Street junction. It closed in 1913 and the street was subsequently widened.

KING STREET 1986

SAFEWAY'S SUPERMARKET, surmounted by a multi-storey car park, now stands on the corner. Although a utilitarian building it is striking in appearance.

KING STREET c. 1860

PATRONS, together with a few too young to be serious drinkers, waiting outside the old Royal Oak public house at 89 King Street. This pub was rebuilt in 1929.

KING STREET 1986

THE NEW Royal Oak closed its doors in 1975 to be replaced by a row of shops and offices. King Street has certainly changed in character, especially on the south side, with the opening of the Stoneborough Centre and several large chain stores.

THE ATTRACTIVE Kent County Ophthalmic Hospital was constructed in 1852 using the locally-quarried hard grey limestone known as ragstone.

ONLY THE parked cars and the absence of chimneys serve to mark the passing of over one hundred years.

THE FORESTERS' ARMS public house was once owned by Isherwood, Foster and Stacey who produced their beer at the Lower Brewery in nearby Water Lane, off Gabriel's Hill. They were subsequently taken over by Fremlins. In 1940 a delayed action bomb fell on the pub and later exploded, wrecking it and killing a bomb disposal officer. *(Photo – Kent Messenger)*

KNIGHTRIDER STREET 1986

AFTER THE Foresters' was destroyed, the brewery acquired a wooden tea shack from Wrotham Hill and erected it as a 'temporary' pub. The pub closed in 1967 but the shack remains and is now occupied by Young Enterprise, an organisation designed to teach business skills to young people.

PUPILS OF THE Maidstone Bluecoat school assembled outside their school building, which had earlier been the local workhouse, erected in 1720. Bluecoat schools were charity schools set up in the 18th century to educate the children of the poor. They were based on the original Bluecoat School of Christ's Hospital, London and as the name suggests the children wore distinctive uniforms.

36

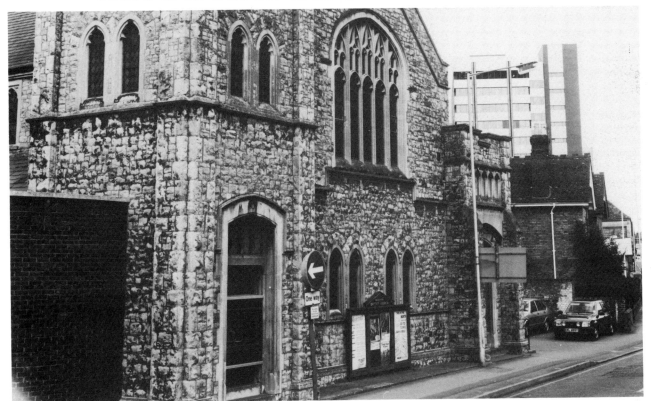

THE BLUECOAT SCHOOL amalgamated with the local grammar schools around 1906; most of the building was demolished and the site was bought by the local Baptists for their new church which opened in 1907. The more recent brick extension on the left of the picture was built on the site of the old Globe Inn.

KNIGHTRIDER STREET 1910

THIS 15TH CENTURY building, known as Mill Farm House had a rendered exterior when this photograph was taken.

REMOVAL OF THE rendering has exposed the attractive timber framing of the house, which is now a wine bar.

KNIGHTRIDER STREET 1905

KNIGHTRIDER HOUSE was the 18th century home of William Shipley, founder of the Royal Society of Arts. It was, until fairly recently the offices of the Maidstone and District Bus Company. Shipley's grave can be seen in nearby All Saints' churchyard.

NOW EMPTY, the listed building is at least secure from major road developments in the area and will probably revert to office use.

MILL STREET 1880

A PHOTOGRAPH taken looking towards the High Street before the weatherboarded Church Mill was demolished in 1902. Church Mill was one of two corn mills in Mill Street. The mill machinery was driven by water flowing from the mill pond on the right hand side of the road. The pond was fed by the river Len, a fast flowing stream which had a number of mills sited on it, including Turkey Mill.

MILL STREET 1986

THE ROAD was apparently widened to accommodate the tram system and the land at the rear of Church Mill was laid out as an addition to Palace Gardens. Most of that area has now vanished under the tarmac of Bishop's Way. Surprisingly the mill pond has survived. Behind it is the showroom of Rootes Ltd, built in 1938, now Talbot dealers. The company was originally part of the Rootes vehicle empire, which had its origins locally.

THE ARCHBISHOP'S STABLES, sometimes known erroneously as the Tithe Barn, was built around 1400 to accommodate the Archbishop of Canterbury's entourage when he broke his journeys to London at his nearby Palace. In 1913 it was bought by public subscription for the town when rumours circulated that it was to be demolished and re-erected in the USA. At the time of this photograph it was being used for munitions work.

MILL STREET 1986

HAVING BEEN SAVED from possible export the building became somewhat of an embarrassment. It was suggested as a possible agricultural museum before the Second World War, and eventually, in 1946 it became the home of Sir Garrard Tyrwhitt-Drake's collection of carriages and horse drawn vehicles. This unusual museum is open throughout the year.

THE MAIDSTONE & District Bus Company's omnibus station on the corner of Palace Avenue and Mill Street opened in 1922. The single storey booking office remained for some years after the station closed, and was eventually dismantled and donated to the Kent and East Sussex railway at Tenterden.

PALACE AVENUE 1986

SHRUBS AND trees now screen a car park and public conveniences. The recent addition to Maidstone Police Station rises above. Law and order is a growth industry in Maidstone today.

ST PETER'S STREET 1911

ST PETER'S STREET was in a busy manufacturing area, leading as it did to the Medway Brewery and gasworks. This photograph shows the offices of Maskell & Son, a local mineral water manufacturer and to the left, the White Swan public house. This, in later years became the Acorn Cafe.

ST PETER'S STREET 1986

TOTALLY unrecognisable now, as four lanes of traffic swing around to the new St Peter's bridge across the Medway. Most of the Medway Brewery was demolished in 1975, although a few buildings remained until fairly recently when the Broadway shopping centre was built. Maskells and the White Swan were approximately where Safeways is now sited.

FLOODING IN WINTER was quite common along Fairmeadow before the installation of improved locks on the River Medway. This photograph taken on 27th December, 1927 shows the floodwater extending up Earl Street, past the Corpus Christi Hall on the left.

EARL STREET 1986

THE BUILDINGS on the riverside have been cleared, giving an unimpeded view of the derelict gasworks site on the opposite bank. Corpus Christi Hall was in mediaeval times the meeting place of a religious guild whose members were prominent citizens and tradesmen. The Corpus Christi Fraternity was dissolved at the time of the Reformation and the town purchased the building for a boys grammar school, which remained there until 1871.   51

UNION STREET c. 1884

THE WESLEYAN Methodist chapel in Union Street, once called Tyler's Lane, was built in 1823 and replaced an earlier chapel dating from 1805. Prior to this the Methodists met in a building on St Faith's Green, which is now part of Brenchley Gardens, adjacent to the museum.

THE GRAVESTONES have been moved back to the boundary walls leaving an expanse of grass in front of the building, which is now decorated in a pleasant pastel green.

ST PAUL'S CHURCH, erected in 1859, had close connections with the Balston family who were the proprietors of Springfield paper mill in nearby Sandling Road. Unfortunately in 1963 children playing with matches caused a fire which completely gutted the building.

INITIALLY St Paul's was to be rebuilt, but the site was later sold for housing and a new church and community hall constructed higher up the Boxley Road. A block of studio apartments occupies the old church site now.

TONBRIDGE ROAD
c . 1 8 8 4

WEST BOROUGH Congregational Church was an imposing ragstone building standing on the corner of Bower Place and Tonbridge Road. It was built in 1875 and had sittings for 423 persons.

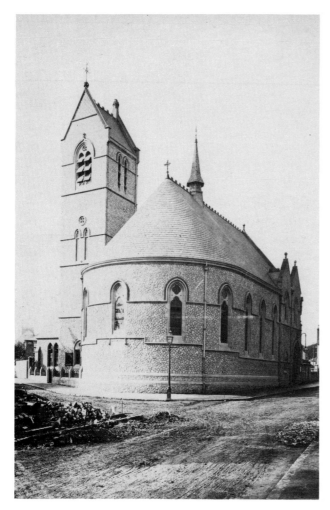

TONBRIDGE ROAD 1986

THE CHURCH amalgamated with two other congregational churches in the 1960s and stayed empty for several years. It was replaced by this block of flats.

COLLEGE ROAD c. 1870

THE OLD ROAD from the south used to pass through the gateway to Archbishop Courtenay's College of Priests, founded in 1395. The early oasthouse, beside the ruined gateway, belonged to College Farm. In the distance is the main College gatehouse, complete with battlements.

COLLEGE ROAD 1986

THIS ROW of almshouses was erected in 1905 by the Cutbush charity. They were originally intended for 'respectable widows or daughters of decayed tradesmen of the town' who had fallen on hard times. Couples are now admitted. The main College buildings behind the almshouses are used by the Kent Music School, having been purchased for the town in 1949 by Sir Garrard Tyrwhitt-Drake.

THESE ATTRACTIVE brick cottages were just below Chillington House, the museum curator's residence, on the site now occupied by the Maidstone Library. There are very few dwellings actually left in the town centre.

THE MAIDSTONE LIBRARY opened in 1964. It is now run by the Kent County Council. Beyond it the gables of Cook Lubbock House can just be seen. This was once an old riverside inn, the Lord Nelson, reputed to be the haunt of smugglers. Even earlier it had been the home of William Weaver, Mayor of Maidstone in 1691 and 1701.

ST FAITH'S STREET c. 1890

AN ORNATE GATEHOUSE to Brenchley Gardens stood above the Museum until 1940 when it was destroyed by the same German bomb which damaged the nearby church. To the right of the gatehouse can be seen the museum tower, built in 1878 to house an astronomical telescope.

ST FAITH'S STREET 1986

MAJOR RESTORATION work at the museum, brought about originally by an arson attack in 1977, is drawing to a close. In the foreground is a modern wishing well, covered by ornate wrought ironwork salvaged from the roof of the old Lower Brewery building which used to stand in Water Lane.

ST FAITH'S STREET c. 1875

ST FAITH'S CHURCH, in nearby Station Road was built in 1871 by E. W. Stephens, a local architect, in ragstone. A square tower, surmounted by four pinnacles, was added in 1882.

ST FAITH'S STREET 1986

A BOMB DROPPED by a German plane in September 1940 demolished the nearby gatehouse to Brenchley Gardens and damaged the tower pinnacles, which were later removed.

BRENCHLEY GARDENS c. 1900

A SMARTLY DRESSED GROUP listens to a string ensemble in front of the bandstand. The gardens commemorate Julius Lucius Brenchley, a local philanthropist and explorer, who donated the land in 1873. St Faith's church tower, complete with pinnacles which were removed during the Second World War can be seen above the trees.

BRENCHLEY GARDENS 1986

ALTHOUGH THE GARDENS are kept immaculately, the bandstand is now seldom used for concerts. In recent years it has served as a platform for rallies in the gardens by such diverse groups as the National Front and striking social workers. It is also a favoured venue for the local break dancing fraternity.

STATION ROAD 1934

THIS OLD Tudor cottage on the corner of St Faith's Street had been a newspaper shop, but in 1934 the living accommodation was condemned as unfit and the property lay empty. It was bought and restored by a local builder, John Bridge, who removed the peg tiles to reveal the timber framing.

STATION ROAD 1986

APPROPRIATELY-NAMED Tudor Cottage hairstylists now occupy the building. The absence of moving vehicles belies the fact that this area carries some of the town's heaviest traffic. The problem will remain until the relief road is constructed from Fairmeadow to Sandling Road.

THE OLD ASSIZE COURTS, designed by Sir Robert Smirke, were built in front of the County Gaol in 1827. They cost £40,000 at that time. The Kent assizes began to be generally held in Maidstone from the beginning of the 17th century. That, together with the town's central position in Kent, contributed to it becoming the county town.

COUNTY ROAD 1986

COUNTY HALL was erected in 1915 in the forecourt of the Assize buildings at a cost of £50,000, indicating inflation was not a serious problem throughout the 19th century. The courts were still held here until the new Law Courts were built near the river. On the left a large office block is being constructed on the former site of the Wig and Gown pub, once called by the rather lengthy name of the New Inn and Railway Hotel.

BROADWAY 1901

CROWDS LINE the Broadway to welcome the West Kent Yeomanry back from the Boer War on the 19th July, 1901. The distinctive arched shop front of George Bunyard can just be seen at the head of the Broadway. Bunyard was a local nurseryman, who specialised in fruit, particularly apples, hence his title of 'pomologist'.

BROADWAY 1986

MAJOR CHANGES have taken place here. The entire right hand side of the street has gone to make way for the Broadway shopping centre, with its mini-Crystal Palace entrance. The other side of the Broadway is also looking 'ripe for redevelopment', as several shops and offices have remained empty for some time now.

BROADWAY c. 1880

A SUNNY DAY on Broadway and the traders have their canvas awnings out to protect the window displays. A man strolls unconcernedly across the road in front of a passing horse and trap. Neither he nor the young lad walking in the gutter would survive long today on this stretch of road.

BROADWAY 1986

APART FROM the Railway Hotel on the right, the scene looks totally different now. The Broadway Centre has replaced the shops and the Law Courts building rises up on the old wood-yard site by the river. This was ear-marked in the 1940s as a suitable position for a civic centre, complete with concert hall, but that was not to be.

BUCKLAND ROAD 1893

GREAT BUCKLAND, an early 17th century manor house, photographed shortly before its demolition. The house formed part of the ancient estate of Buckland, which derived its name from a former tenant, Allan de Bocland. De Bocland was granted the land by the Archbishop of Canterbury during the reign of King John.

THE GRAMMAR SCHOOL for Girls was founded in 1887 and occupied premises in Albion Place for many years. The new school buildings were built approximately on the site of Great Buckland in 1938.

PUDDING LANE c. 1890

THESE OLD HOUSES stood on the corner of Pudding Lane and Earl Street. The name Pudding Lane first appears in a deed dated 1485. The houses were demolished in 1897.

A NEW BRICK FRONTAGE was built onto the exposed building in Earl Street, forming a block which for some years was the estates office of Fremlin's Brewery on the opposite side of the road. It is now a solicitor's office.

PUDDING LANE c. 1926

PUDDING LANE was a much narrower street then. The building with the corrugated roof and flagpole was the Pavilion Picture House, which later became the Ritz cinema. This was destroyed by fire in 1954. The square brick building to the right was the retail department of Fremlin's Brewery at that time.

THE CINEMA was not rebuilt, and was replaced by Cornwallis House, a glass and brick office block, notorious at one time as the home of the local Tax Inspectorate.

CASTLE ROAD c. 1880

ALLINGTON CASTLE stands on the town's outskirts. It was once the home of Sir Thomas Wyatt, who led the unsuccessful rebellion in 1554 against the projected marriage of Queen Mary with Philip II of Spain. Wyatt was beheaded on Tower Hill and the castle forfeited. By the 19th century it had become a derelict ruin.

CASTLE ROAD 1986

LORD CONWAY purchased the Castle ruins in 1905 and spent over twenty years restoring the building to its former state. It is now home for a community of Carmelite friars and is regularly opened to the public.

ONE OF the most picturesque areas around Maidstone is the 'secret' valley of Loose, which was once important for its cloth fulling mills. Most of these were converted to paper mills and the Bockingford Arms public house served beer to the thirsty workforce. Its earlier name, The Hand in Hand, re-inforces this connection since the clasped handshake was the emblem of the Original Society of Papermakers.

THE PUB is now a private house and the weatherboarded agricultural building in the foreground has become a row of cottages. The Barcham Green family still operate one of the country's last hand-made papermills a little further down the valley towards Tovil.

THE PHOTOGRAPHER must have set his tripod up on this stack of timber in Smythe's wood-yard to get this shot of the bridge, which was taken shortly after the bridge was built.

MAIDSTONE BRIDGE 1986

LUNCHTIME SHOPPERS stroll back from the Tuesday market via Jubilee Walk named in celebration of the Queen's silver jubilee in 1977. The bridge itself looks much the same as in the previous photograph but both Town and Bridge wharves have gone. The recently erected and somewhat controversial Bridge clock can be seen on the far side.

UNDERCLIFFE c. 1875

'UNDER THE CLIFF' as it appears on the older maps, runs below the Archbishop's Palace. The old five arched bridge in the distance was demolished in 1879, just after the new bridge, designed by Sir Joseph Bazalgette, had been opened.

UNDERCLIFFE 1986

STILL A pleasant place to read the newspaper, doze in the sun, or watch the river activities. Leisure use of the river is actively encouraged by the local council, culminating in a River Festival in July.

RIVER MEDWAY 1877

THIS VIEW of the old bridge was obviously taken from a boat in mid-river. To the left is Fairmeadow, which in earlier times had been an open space used by the townspeople for recreation. By this date it had been macadamised and was being used for the stock markets. On the other bank is Albion Wharf. Part of the Medway Brewery can be seen on the extreme right.

RIVER MEDWAY 1986

THE REMOVAL of the electricity works from Fairmeadow means that the area can again be used for recreation. The opposite bank is also open space. The dominant feature is now the Law Courts building on the far side of the bridge, although the Ferryman Tavern with its pointed roofs, perhaps reminiscent of a group of Kentish oast houses, can hardly fail to catch the eye.

RIVER MEDWAY c. 1880

A BEAUTIFULLY composed and executed photograph taken from the bridge. On the far bank the Palace chimneys and All Saints tower rise above the trees. In the foreground a cluster of sailing barges moored at the woodyard demonstrate how important the river was in those days for the transport of heavy goods.

VERY LITTLE has changed on the far bank but the new Law Courts have certainly made an impression over on the south-west bank. They were officially opened by Her Majesty the Queen on 31st October, 1984.

RIVER MEDWAY c. 1900

A BIRD'S EYE VIEW of industrial Maidstone, photographed from the Iguanodon corn mill, downstream of the old High Level rail bridge. On the far bank, approximately in the centre of the photograph is the Waterside brewery of E. Mason. The chimney of Fremlins Brewery can be seen slightly to the right. Drayson's timber yard at Baltic Wharf later became Tilling-Steven's Victoria Works.

RIVER MEDWAY 1986

MOST OF WATERSIDE is now clear of buildings in preparation for the planned road extension, the exception being the old Waterside Granary which is now the Warehouse nightclub. The Tilling-Steven's factory closed in 1977, the victim of takeovers in the motor industry. The only remaining major manufacturer in the town centre is Trebor-Sharp Ltd, who occupy the large building centre right.

DO YOU ENJOY VIEWING OLD PHOTOGRAPHS?

The Maidstone Museum has an excellent collection of photographs which record the history of the town and its development over the last 120 years. There are gaps and the collection must not be allowed to stand still. Today's snapshot is tomorrow's history. If you have any old or recent photographs with local connections (not necessarily street views) the staff would be pleased to see them. So might future generations of Maidstonians. I hope you will contact us.

R.S.

OTHER KENT TITLES
AVAILABLE FROM COUNTRYSIDE BOOKS

Smuggling in Kent & Sussex 1700–1840	*Mary Waugh*
The Kent Village Book	*Alan Bignell*
Tales of Old Kent	*Alan Bignell*
Country Ways in Kent	*Anthony Howard*

For a complete catalogue please write to:
Countryside Books
3 Catherine Road
Newbury
Berkshire RG14 7NA